Han

The Mother who Prayed

The Story of Hannah
Accurately retold from the Bible
(from the book of 1 Samuel)
by Carine Mackenzie

Illustrations by
Duncan McLaren
Cover design by Danie van Straaten

Published in Great Britain by
Christian Focus Publications Ltd
Geanies House, Fearn, Tain, Ross-shire, IV20 1TW, Scotland.
www.christianfocus.com
© copyright 1983 Christian Focus Publications Ltd
ISBN 1-84550-163-2

New edition 1988
Reprinted 1991
Reprinted 2006

Hannah lived in the country of Israel many years ago. She was married to a good man called Elkanah and they lived in the town of Ramah. In those days some good men had more than one wife. Elkanah had another wife called Peninnah who had several sons and daughters.

Hannah's greatest sorrow was that she did not have a child. How she longed to have a baby son of her own.

Every year Elkanah took his family to Shiloh to worship the Lord God in his temple.

God wants us also to worship him, both in church and at home, by singing praise to him, reading the Bible and praying to him.

Each year, at Shiloh, Elkanah gave gifts to all his family. Peninnah and her boys and girls all received a gift but Hannah received a special gift because he loved her best of all.

No gift could make Hannah forget that she did not have a child of her own. Peninnah mocked her for not having any children. This made poor Hannah feel even more miserable. You may know just how Hannah felt. It can be very upsetting to have someone mocking you.

Hannah could not eat her food and often cried. Not even Elkanah, who loved her so much, could comfort her.

'Why are you crying?' he asked her. 'Why do you not take something to eat? Why are you so sad? Am I not better to you than ten sons could be?'

But Elkanah could not really help
her with her problem. Hannah
knew that the only one who could
help her was the Lord God.

One day, when they were in Shiloh, Hannah made her way alone to the temple of the Lord. She felt very sad. In the temple she wept and prayed and told all her problems to the Lord.

In her prayer, she made a promise to the Lord: 'If you will remember me and give me a baby boy, I will give him back to work for the Lord for all his life.'

While Hannah was praying
Eli the priest was sitting on
a seat by a pillar of the temple.
He noticed Hannah and watched
her closely. He thought she
looked very strange. As she
prayed in her heart, her
lips moved but no sound
came from her mouth, so
Eli thought she had drunk
too much wine. He went
to Hannah and said to her,
'How long are you going
to be drunk? Stop drinking
so much wine!' Hannah
turned to him and said, 'I am
a very sad woman. I have not
been drinking wine at all. I am
in great distress and have been
telling the Lord all about it.'

Eli realised his mistake and said to her, 'Go away in peace and may God give you what you have asked for.'

'I hope you will always think kindly of me,' Hannah replied.

Hannah believed that God would answer her prayer and she went back to the house very happy indeed. She did not look sad any more. She felt so much better that she began to eat her food again.

What a difference it had made to Hannah to tell her problem to the Lord God. Today too you can take your problems to God. You can tell him all your worries because he asks you to do so. He promises to help you if you trust in him.

The next day Elkanah and his family rose early in the morning. They went to the temple to worship the Lord. Then they set off back to their own home in Ramah.

After some time Hannah had a baby son of her own and she was very happy indeed. God had answered her prayer. Hannah did not forget that she had asked God for this baby, for she called him Samuel. Samuel means 'asked of God.'

The next time that Elkanah went to Shiloh to worship the Lord, Hannah did not go with him. 'I will stay at home with Samuel,' she said to her husband. 'I will take him to Shiloh when he is a little older. Then I will give him to the Lord and he will stay there always.' Elkanah agreed with Hannah. 'Yes,' he said, 'you do what you think best. Wait until Samuel is old enough.'

So when Samuel was a little older, Hannah took him to the house of the Lord in Shiloh. Hannah went to Eli the priest and reminded him of their last meeting. 'I am the woman that you saw praying here to the Lord. I prayed for this child and the Lord gave me what I asked for. I am now keeping my promise and returning the child to work for the Lord.'

So Samuel stayed in the temple with Eli from that day on. He learned to help Eli, who was an old man, with many little tasks.

He also worshipped God in the temple. We must not think that it is only grown-up people who have to worship God. Boys and girls also must worship Him.

When Hannah was in trouble, you remember, she prayed to God to help her. Now that she was happy, she did not forget God. She prayed again telling him how happy and joyful she felt. She knew that God was holy and great and strong. She also praised God and said, 'There is no one so great as God. God has made the whole world and rules over everyone.'

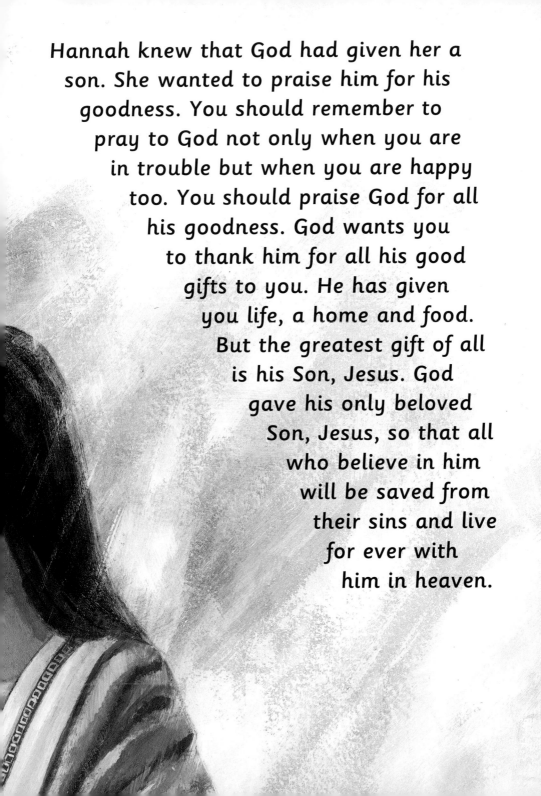

Hannah knew that God had given her a son. She wanted to praise him for his goodness. You should remember to pray to God not only when you are in trouble but when you are happy too. You should praise God for all his goodness. God wants you to thank him for all his good gifts to you. He has given you life, a home and food. But the greatest gift of all is his Son, Jesus. God gave his only beloved Son, Jesus, so that all who believe in him will be saved from their sins and live for ever with him in heaven.

Elkanah and Hannah went back to Ramah. They left Samuel at Shiloh with Eli. He worked for the Lord there, just as his mother had promised.

Each year after that Hannah still went with Elkanah to Shiloh to worship in the house of the Lord. How she would look forward to seeing Samuel again. Every time she went she brought him a little coat that she had made for him.

Hannah willingly gave her son to work for God, but she was not left without any children at home. God rewarded her by giving her more children: three boys and two girls.

You will remember that Hannah's prayer for her son was that he would serve the Lord in the temple. This prayer was answered too. Day by day Samuel served God in the temple and was a true servant of God. God soon showed that he loved Samuel.

One evening Eli, who was now nearly blind, went to bed as usual. After he had finished his tasks, young Samuel also went to bed. As he lay there, all of a sudden he heard a voice calling his name.

He thought that it was Eli who was calling him, 'Here I am,' he answered, as he ran to Eli. 'You were calling me.'

'I did not call you,' Eli replied. 'Go back to bed again.'

Again he heard someone calling 'Samuel!' Samuel rose again and went to Eli. 'Here I am,' he said, 'for you did call me.'

'I did not call you,' said Eli. 'Lie down again.'

God was calling to Samuel but Samuel did not know this.

Samuel heard the voice again calling his name for the third time. 'Here I am for you did call me,' he said to Eli.

This time Eli knew that the voice that Samuel was hearing was the voice of God. 'Go and lie down,' Eli said to Samuel, 'and if he calls you again say, "Speak Lord for your servant is listening."'

God did speak to Samuel again. He told him that Eli's sons were very wicked. Eli did not punish them or stop them, so the whole family was to be punished.

Samuel lay in bed, thinking about what had happened. In the morning he rose as usual to open the big doors of the temple, but was afraid to tell Eli what God had said to him.

But Eli called for Samuel and asked him what God had said. 'Do not hide anything from me,' he urged the boy. Samuel told him everything. Eli's humble reply was, 'It is the Lord; let him do what seems best to him.'

Hannah's son served the Lord as a young boy and when he grew up he continued serving the Lord.

Samuel became an important man of God: all in answer to his mother's prayers. Hannah loved God so much that she did not keep her son for herself. She was a woman with a problem but she prayed to God about that problem. God helped her. God is still the same today. He tells you to take your problems to Him.